COUNTRIES IN OUR WORLD

CHINA

Oliver James

FRANKLIN WATTS
LONDON•SYDNEY

First published in 2009 by
Franklin Watts
338 Euston Road
London NW1 3BH

Franklin Watts Australia
Level 17/207 Kent Street
Sydney NSW 2000

 Produced for Franklin Watts by White-Thomson
Publishing Ltd
+44 (0) 845 362 8240
www.wtpub.co.uk

Series consultant: Rob Bowden
Editor: Sonya Newland
Designer: Hayley Cove
Picture researcher: Rob Bowden

A CIP catalogue record for this book is available from
the British Library.

Dewey Classification: 915.1

ISBN 978 0 7496 8843 1

Printed in Malaysia

Franklin Watts is a division of Hachette Children's Books, an
Hachette UK company. www.hachette.co.uk

Picture Credits
Corbis: 8 (Chen Fei/Xinhua Press), 9 (China Newsphoto/
Reuters), 15 (Lynsey Addario), 19 (Xu Yu/Xinhua Press), 21
(Xiaoyang Liu), 26 (epa). **EASI-Images:** Adrian Cooper 4, 12,
13, 14, 16, 18, 20, 24, 27, 29 / Tony Binns 6,
17, 22, 23 / Rob Bowden 7. **Photoshot:** 10 (CNImaging).
Shutterstock: 11 (Holger Mette), 25 (Sam DCruz), 28 (rodho).

Contents

Introducing China   4

Landscapes and environment   8

Population and migration   12

Culture and lifestyles   16

Economy and trade   20

Government and politics   24

China in 2020   28

Glossary   30

Further information   31

Index   32

Introducing China

China is the fourth biggest country in the world and it has the largest population. In 2008, almost one in every five people on Earth lived in China. For much of the last century, China was quite isolated and had little impact on the rest of the world. This began to change in the 1970s, and China is now one of the most important and powerful countries in the world.

▼ *Shanghai has always been a global city. It is now leading the rest of China towards becoming one of the world's superpowers.*

▲ *China, along with Russia, has 14 international land borders – more than any other country in the world.*

A new world power

In 2007, China became the fourth richest country in the world. It is now richer than the UK and France, and only Germany, Japan and the USA are wealthier. China has some of the world's biggest companies, and its factories produce goods for export across the globe. In fact, China is so successful that you are probably wearing something made in China right now, or you will almost certainly use something made in China during your day.

Faster and faster

As well as having a new global importance, there have also been great changes within China itself. The size of its cities, the number of cars on its roads and the wealth of its people are all growing faster than in almost any other country in the world. From 2000, China's economy grew three to four times faster than that of countries such as the USA or the UK. This growth began to slow down dramatically in 2008, though, as an economic crisis hit countries all over the world.

▲ *This man is making paper in the same way that it was made in China over 2,000 years ago.*

IT STARTED HERE

Paper

The Chinese first invented paper-making around 2,200 years ago. It was commonly used for writing by around 1,700 years ago. By about 1,500 years ago it was even being used as toilet paper!

China in need

China's growth has been so rapid that it cannot meet all its own needs. It does not have enough of many basic resources, such as timber and steel, which are needed for building or as raw materials for industry, so it must import these items from other countries. China is one of the world's biggest consumers of resources. In 2006, it was estimated that half of all the trees cut down in the world were used by China. And in 2008, China used nearly one-third of all the steel produced in the world.

China and the world

Today China has a major influence on the rest of the world – its use of steel, for example, has led to shortages in other countries. But China has been influencing the world for hundreds, even thousands of years. Many things we use or enjoy originally came from China, including fireworks, kite-flying, silk, pasta, umbrellas, paper money and the compass.

BASIC DATA

Official name: **People's Republic of China**

Capital: **Beijing**

Size: **9,596,960 sq km (3,705,407 sq miles)**

Population: **1,330,044,605**

Currency: **Yuan (¥)**

Chinese around the world

Another way that China influences the world is in the spread of its people. Chinese communities can now be found across the globe, and the Chinese people have taken their customs and culture with them. Chinese food, for example, is now one of the world's most popular foods.

▼ *A dragon-dance team takes part in a Chinese New Year celebration in Sydney, Australia. Sydney has a large Chinese population.*

China is so large that each area of the country has a different landscape and environment. In the north and west China is high and dry, but in the south and east it is lower and wetter. China's mountains, rivers, deserts and coasts are among the largest on Earth.

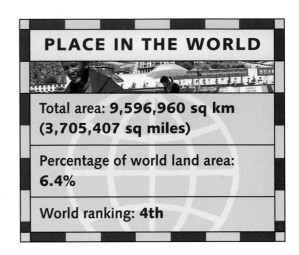

PLACE IN THE WORLD

Total area: **9,596,960 sq km (3,705,407 sq miles)**	
Percentage of world land area: **6.4%**	
World ranking: **4th**	

The roof of the world

The highest part of China is the Tibetan Plateau. It covers an enormous area of land – almost four times bigger than France. Most of the Plateau is over 4,000 to 5,000 m (13,100 to 16,400 ft) above sea level. This is higher than Mont Blanc, the tallest mountain in Western Europe. The Plateau is very cold for most of the year and few people live there. Lhasa is the main city in the region.

▼ *The Potala Palace dominates Lhasa, the capital of Tibet and the main settlement on the vast Tibetan Plateau.*

 Visitors watch the Hukou Waterfall on the Yellow River. The colour – and the river's name – comes from sediment in the water.

IT'S A FACT!

Mount Everest, which lies on the border between China and Nepal, is the world's highest mountain at 8,850 m (29,035 ft) above sea level. China also shares the world's second highest mountain with Pakistan. It is called K2 and stands 8,611 m (28,251 ft) above sea level.

Rivers of China

China's most important river, the Yangtze – or Chang Jiang as it is called in China – begins on the Tibetan Plateau. From there it crosses the country and joins the East China Sea near Shanghai. At 6,300 km (3,915 miles) it is the third longest river in the world. It is important for transport and trade, and the land around the river produces nearly half of China's crops. Nearly one-third of China's people live along its path. The Yellow River (Huang He) is China's other main river and is 5,464 km (3,395 miles) long. It also starts on the Tibetan Plateau and flows across northern China to the Yellow Sea.

Deserts of the north

China has two major deserts. The Gobi Desert lies along the border with Mongolia and is a mainly rocky desert. It has been growing since the 1950s and is now less than 80 km (50 miles) from Beijing. The Takla Makan Desert is in north-west China and is about the size of Italy. It is one of the largest sandy deserts in the world: in some places the sand is 300 m (1,000 ft) deep! No one lives in the Takla Makan Desert because strong winds there cause sand storms almost every day of the year.

◀ *A man wades through Zhangzhou city in June 2008 after storms led to localized flooding. An early-warning system meant that few people were harmed, but many properties were damaged.*

Natural hazards

Flooding has killed millions of people in China over the last 150 years, especially on the Yellow and Yangtze rivers. Tropical storms can damage settlements along the coast, but early-warning systems and shelters mean that few people are killed. Earthquakes are much harder to predict. In 2008, a major earthquake hit Sichuan province in the centre of China, killing 70,000 people and making more than four million homeless.

IT'S A FACT!

The Yellow River is known in China as the 'river of sorrow' because it has the record for the worst floods of all time. In 1887, the river burst its banks and killed up to 2.5 million people. It flooded again in 1931, killing an estimated one to two million people, making it easily the deadliest river in the world.

Endangered wildlife

China's fast growth has harmed many natural environments. Rivers and forests have been especially damaged by industry, farming and transport. Pandas have lost large areas of their natural bamboo forests, and the rare Yangtze River dolphin may already be extinct. Scientists could not find a single one after searching for six weeks in 2007.

▼ *The giant panda is one of China's most endangered species and has become a symbol of conservation work worldwide. These pandas are at a breeding centre in Chengdu.*

GLOBAL LEADER

Hydroelectric Power (HEP)
China's Three Gorges Dam across the Yangtze River is the world's biggest HEP dam. When it is finished in 2011, it will produce the same amount of electricity as 15 coal-powered stations. However, the lake created by the dam will force thousands of people to leave their homes, and there are also concerns about the impact the dam will have on local wildlife.

China has more people living in it than any other country. In fact, if the global population was just 100 people then 20 of them would be from China. This is compared to 17 from India, 4.5 from the USA and less than one from the UK.

PLACE IN THE WORLD

Population:	**1,330,044,605**
Percentage of world total:	**19.9%**
World ranking:	**1st**

Growing fast

In 1900, China had around 430 million people but this increased to 555 million by 1950. In the second half of the twentieth century, improvements in healthcare helped the population grow even faster. By 1981, it had passed one billion and by 2000, China had an amazing 1.26 billion people. This means that between 1950 and 2000, China's population increased by about 27 people every minute! It has slowed down since then, but is still growing by around 16 people a minute.

▶ *China is constantly building to keep pace with its enormous and fast-growing population.*

Too many people

When a population grows quickly it can be difficult to keep up with the need for food, water, housing, healthcare and education. In 1979, China decided to solve this problem by limiting each family to just one child. These one-child families would be well cared for by the government. However, if people chose to have larger families, they would be fined or could even lose their jobs.

The one-child policy

By 2008, China said that its one-child policy had reduced population growth by at least 300 million people. This is about the same as the entire population of the USA! One problem with the policy is that there are now around 117 boys for every 100 girls in China. Parents would rather have a boy, and many have chosen not to keep the baby if they find out it is a girl.

GOING GLOBAL

China has one of the largest overseas populations of any country. Between 35 and 60 million Chinese people live outside China, mostly in other Asian countries or in North America and Europe. The USA has around three million Chinese and the UK has around 300,000.

▶ *A grandfather stands with his granddaughter. It is common in China for grandparents to care for children while their parents are out working.*

China's growing cities

In 1950, most Chinese people lived in rural areas and only 13 in every 100 people lived in towns or cities. Since then, China's urban areas have grown very quickly, and by 2008 they were home to around 43 per cent of the population. China has some of the largest cities in the world. Shanghai has around 15.5 million people and Beijing around 11.5 million. In total, China has 109 cities with a population of more than one million, compared to 42 in the USA and only five in the UK.

Leaving China

Every year, an estimated one to two million people leave China in search of work. They follow others, and there are now Chinese communities in over 140 countries. In many places, Chinese migrants choose to live together in one community. They have their own restaurants and shops specializing in Chinese food and other goods. In cities such as London, New York and Sydney, these areas are known as 'Chinatown'.

◀ *As China's cities grow, many older structures are being demolished to make way for new and bigger buildings to house even more people.*

IT'S A FACT!

The number of people living in China's towns and cities is almost double the entire population of the USA or nearly 10 times the population of the UK!

▲ *Chinese workers oversee the construction of a new railway in Angola, Africa. Chinese labourers are involved in similar projects around the world.*

Overseas labour

China has many skilled workers who can offer expertise to other countries at a low cost. Chinese companies and workers have become global leaders in large construction projects, for example. In Africa they have built many roads, railways, dams and bridges. In the Caribbean they have been building government offices and sports stadiums such as the new Antigua and Barbuda stadium, which was built for the 2007 Cricket World Cup.

GLOBAL LEADER

Dongtan Eco-city

By 2010, China hopes to open the world's first environmentally friendly city, on an island in the Yangtze River. Dongtan Eco-city will provide homes and work for around 10,000 people. Energy will come from the wind, sun, biofuels and recycled waste. Public transport will use clean fuels and people will be encouraged to cycle and walk. Farms will produce organic food for the city and take away waste for turning into compost.

Over the centuries, China's ancient and fascinating culture has spread all around the world, as well as being closely linked to the way Chinese people lived. This is changing now, though, as China is having to balance traditions with new ideas and influences coming from other parts of the world.

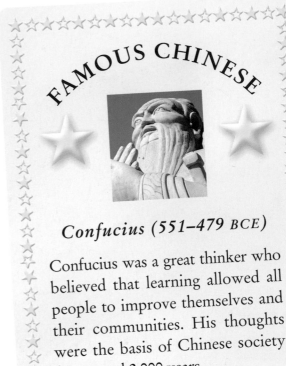

FAMOUS CHINESE

Confucius (551–479 BCE)

Confucius was a great thinker who believed that learning allowed all people to improve themselves and their communities. His thoughts were the basis of Chinese society for around 2,000 years.

Religion and beliefs

China has been an important centre of religious beliefs for hundreds of years. Confucianism and Daoism (Taoism) are especially important, and had a big influence on Chinese rulers. In the twentieth century, religion was restricted because the government believed it threatened its control. People now have greater religious freedom, but some beliefs, such as Falun Gong, are still banned. The main religions in China are Confucianism, Daoism and Buddhism, with a smaller number following Islam or Christianity. About 40 per cent of Chinese say they have no religion at all.

▶ *Confucius is one of China's most important historical figures. His ideas about how we should live have influenced people around the world.*

▲ *Villagers bathe their buffalo in front of their rice paddies. This is typical of many rural villages, where life has changed little in hundreds of years.*

Growing up in China

A child growing up in one of China's cities will have a very different life from a child growing up in rural China. In the cities most people live in apartment blocks, but in rural areas families live in simple one-storey, two-room houses with animals grazing outside. City life is made easier with technology such as computers and modern appliances such as fridges and washing machines. In rural areas people are less likely to have these, and instead have the basic equipment needed to grow crops and look after animals.

THE HOME OF...

Traditional Chinese Medicine

Traditional Chinese medicine has been practised in China for over 3,000 years. Illnesses such as skin complaints, fevers and throat infections are treated using mixtures of dried plant, mineral and animal ingredients. Chinese medicine is now popular with non-Chinese people around the world as an alternative to Western drugs. Chinese medicine has been criticized for encouraging a trade in rare animals whose body parts are believed to have special properties. These include rhino horn and tiger bones.

Feeding the people

Food is an important part of cultural life in China, but feeding 1.3 billion people is also a major challenge. Rice is China's main food and has been grown there for over 8,000 years. Although modern rice-farming machinery has been introduced, many small farms still use animal power and farm rice by hand. China exports only around one per cent of its rice, but it produces so much that it is still the world's sixth largest exporter.

IT STARTED HERE

Pasta

Pasta is often thought of as Italian, but a 4,000-year-old bowl of noodles found in China shows that the Chinese were probably the first to invent pasta-making.

◀ *Street food, such as that served at this chow-mein stall, is popular. More unusual offerings include deep-fried scorpions or grasshoppers!*

Changing diets

As people become richer and new tastes arrive from outside the country, Chinese diets are changing. Traditionally, most people would eat either rice or noodles with vegetables, with small amounts of meat or fish as a side dish. A more Western-style diet, with more meat, fish and dairy products, and higher levels of fat and sugar, is now common in China. This has made the Chinese people fatter, too. Since 1990, the number of overweight or obese people has almost trebled to around 325 million in 2008.

Health and sport

Personal fitness is important to Chinese people. In large cities across the country, people gather each morning to practise a traditional type of exercise and martial art called tai chi chuan. Other martial arts, including judo and karate, are also popular. Badminton, diving and table tennis are among China's most successful sports. Imported sports such as football and basketball have become popular, too.

THE HOME OF...

Chinese Astrology

Chinese astrology follows a 12-year cycle, with each year named after its own animal. Astrologers believe that someone's personality depends on which animal sign they were born under. The 12 animals are: rat, tiger, dragon, horse, monkey, dog, ox, rabbit, snake, sheep, rooster and pig.

▲ *Wang Liqin won a gold medal in table tennis at the 2008 Olympics in Beijing. Table tennis is one of the most popular sports in China.*

GLOBAL LEADER

Olympics 2008

In 2008, the Chinese capital Beijing hosted the 29th Olympic Games. The Chinese team won more gold medals than any other nation, taking 51 of the 302 gold medals awarded.

Economy and trade

China's economy has grown so quickly that it has often been called an economic miracle. In the 1960s, China had very little international trade, but today goods made in China are sold in almost every corner of the world.

◀ *Women working in the service sector – in a shop that sells CDs and DVDs. China now produces such items for the global market.*

Open for business

In 1978, the Chinese government decided to open the economy to greater trade with other countries. They set up special areas where foreign companies could build factories and where goods could be imported and exported. As trade increased, China's economy began to grow and by 1990 the wealth of the country had almost doubled.

IT STARTED HERE

Banknotes

It is thought that banknotes were first used in ancient China in around 800 CE. During a shortage of copper, the emperor at the time allowed paper notes to be issued in exchange for cash. Because they were lighter than coins, the idea caught on, and within 100 years paper money was used all over China. Early Chinese banknotes had coins printed on them to remind people who couldn't read what the note was for!

It just keeps growing

By 2008, the Chinese economy was 8.8 times bigger than it had been in 1990. By comparison, the world's biggest economy – the USA – grew by just 2.4 times in the same period. The world economy slowed in 2008, but in China it is still predicted to grow at around nine per cent. This is mainly because of the country's lead role in global trade, with more and more goods being 'made in China'.

▼ *An excursion boat passes in front of Pudong in Shanghai, China's main financial district and a global symbol of China's rapid economic growth.*

Changing economy

As China's economy has grown, its structure has also changed. In 1990, agriculture was responsible for about 27 per cent of China's economy, but by 2007 this had fallen to just 11 per cent. As farming has decreased in importance for the economy, industry and manufacturing have increased. They made up almost half of the economy in 2007. The other growing area is services, which include trade, transport, retail and other areas such as banking, insurance, healthcare and education. These now make up around 40 per cent of the economy.

▲ *Farming is still labour intensive in many parts of China, especially at key times such as harvest. These people are separating wheat grain from the waste after it has been harvested.*

Work, work, work

Chinese people are extremely hard-working, but this is sometimes abused by companies that make people work long hours for low wages. Long working hours are also blamed for the high number of accidents at Chinese factories, mines and building sites. Farming is still the biggest employer in China, but more and more people are leaving to try and find factory or office jobs in the cities. Some will even leave China to find work and send money home to their families. In 2007, Chinese workers living overseas sent US$25.7 billion back home to their families – more than any other country except India.

IT'S A FACT!

China has the world's biggest workforce, with over 800 million people in 2007. This is greater than the entire population of the USA and the European Union combined!

Trade, trade, trade

The import and export of goods and services made up nearly three-quarters of China's economy in 2007. Its main exports are manufactured goods such as toys, electronic items, tools and textiles. It is estimated that Chinese factories make around 50 per cent of the world's computers, 60 per cent of its digital cameras and 65 per cent of all mobile phones! Most of these are made in China for foreign companies, but Chinese companies are now growing, too. By 2008, there were over 5,000 Chinese companies with business investments in 172 countries and regions around the world.

PLACE IN THE WORLD

Value of economy:
US$3,120,891,000,000

Percentage of world total: 5.9%

World ranking: 4th

▼ *Tourism is one of China's fastest-growing trades. In 2007, 55 million visitors spent US$42 billion. The Great Wall of China is the most popular tourist attraction.*

Buying the world

China's enormous population and growing economy is very demanding. The construction of new buildings, for example, means that China was using about 46 per cent of the world's cement by 2006. The biggest concern, however, is over food. In early 2008, world food shortages and rising prices were blamed partly on China's growing demand for food. As incomes increase and diets change, this demand will increase even more. Some experts are worried that this could have a major impact on other countries, especially poorer ones without the economic power that China has.

China has one of the oldest civilizations on Earth, but by the early twentieth century its leadership was weak from years of war and conflict. In 1949, a new China emerged and was named the People's Republic of China. It was the start of communist rule in China and began a period of incredible change that continues today.

FAMOUS CHINESE

Mao Zedong (1893–1976)

Mao Zedong is often called 'the father of modern China'. His leadership was not all good, though. In 1958 he introduced new farming plans that led to a massive famine that killed 20 million people.

Total control

Communism is where the government has total control over the way in which a country is run. Where people live and work, what they learn and eat, and even when they can marry, are all decided by the government. China's first communist leader, Mao Zedong, introduced many controls when he came to power in 1954, and banned all opposition to the government. He was also very suspicious of Western countries such as the UK and USA, and so for many years China was more or less cut off from the rest of the world.

▶ *A portrait of Mao Zedong, China's most influential leader of recent times, hangs on the palace known as the Forbidden City in Beijing.*

Land arguments

Modern China includes areas of land that others say do not belong to China. The most famous is Tibet, which was occupied by the Chinese in 1950. In 1959, the spiritual leader of Tibet, the Dalai Lama, was forced to leave, and Tibet became an official region of China in 1965. Since then, many organizations have campaigned asking China to free Tibet and let the Tibetan people rule themselves once again. The Free Tibet movement is an international campaign that has supporters all over the world.

▲ *These people in Vancouver, Canada, are protesting against the Chinese occupation of Tibet.*

IT'S A FACT!

The Chinese government employs more than 10 million officials. This is far more than in any other country, and is greater than the population of many countries!

Looking out

The death of Mao Zedong in 1976 marked a change in China's relationship with the world. By 1978, China had agreed a new political friendship with the USA, and agreements with other countries soon followed. China's main reason for building such relationships is to help its own trade and industry.

▼ *China's President Hu Jintao (left) and his Sudanese counterpart Omar Hassan al-Bashir (right) shake hands at a meeting in Sudan, at which China promised greater links with Sudan.*

China and Africa

Since 2000, China has been building new political friendships with Africa. African countries have large reserves of energy and other resources that China needs. In return for supplies of oil, copper and other resources, China is giving African leaders billions of dollars in aid. Although this is good for China, the country has been criticized for giving aid to countries where there is war or conflict. This is because of fears that the money is being used for fighting instead of development in countries such as Sudan and Zimbabwe.

Human rights

China may have opened up to the world, but it is still very strict with its own people. Criminals in China can be executed for crimes such as stealing petrol or avoiding taxes, for example. The Chinese government also controls media such as newspapers and television, and it decides which websites the Chinese people can access. Some people believe that this is a violation of human and civil rights.

▲ *A Chinese news reporter filming on location in Beijing. The government is criticized for its strict control over the media.*

GOING GLOBAL

In 2006, trade between Africa and China was worth around US$30 billion – six times more than in 2000. By 2010 it is expected to increase to over US$100 billion.

Global superpower

China is one of only five permanent members of the United Nations (UN) Security Council. This is the most important part of the UN and is responsible for keeping global peace. This gives China great power in world affairs, but its growing economic wealth makes it even more powerful. Some experts believe that China could soon pass the USA to become the most powerful country in the world.

Since China began to open up to the world in 1978, its economy has grown by around 9.5 per cent every year. Few other countries can match this, but what will China do in the future? Some believe it has grown too fast and will collapse, but others see no end to China's incredible success.

▼ *A new luxury housing development in south-east China. These houses are aimed at China's new rich as homes or holiday homes.*

Business as usual

If China's economy continues to grow as it has since 1978, it is likely that by 2020 it will have passed the USA as the world's richest country. It will have passed Japan and Germany by 2015. But not everything will be easy for China. Its population will have grown to around 1.42 billion and 53 per cent of them (756 million) will live in towns and cities. China will need several cities like Dongtan (see page 15) if it is to support this increase without destroying its already delicate environment.

▲ *More and more Chinese are becoming wealthy enough to shop in modern fashion stores. It is a symbol of the new, twenty-first century China.*

Future changes

Although China has been catching up with Western countries, it will need to find new ways to develop in the future. Using more renewable energy will reduce its impact on the environment and limit pollution. The government may also need to scrap the one-child policy, as there are concerns that China will not have enough young people to care for its ageing population. At the moment there is only one child for every two parents and four grandparents!

China in the world

If everyone in China chose to live in the same way as an average American or European by the year 2020, then it would have a major impact on the world. Changes in diet would mean there was a shortage of food, and greater energy use would lead to global fuel shortages. But China and its people have a right to develop. The solution is for China – and all countries – to make lifestyle choices that allow everyone to benefit more equally in the future.

Glossary

astrology the study of the influence of the stars, planets, sun and moon on human affairs.

biofuels fuels that come from recently dead materials, usually plants, instead of fossil fuels such as coal.

Buddhism a religion that follows the teachings of Buddha (c. 563-483 BCE), and involves studying wisdom, meditation and following an ethical code.

Christianity a religion that follows the teachings of Jesus Christ.

Communism the political and social system in countries with a ruling Communist Party, where all property is owned by the state. Food and supplies are given out to the people.

Confucianism a philosophy or way of life based around the teachings of Confucius (551-479 BCE).

conservation looking after the natural environment and wildlife.

Daoism a system of philosophical beliefs that focuses on an ethical code and encourages compassion towards others.

economy the financial system of a country or region, including how much money is made from the production and sale of goods and services.

export to send or transport products or materials abroad for sale or trade.

Falun Gong a spiritual movement that began in China in the late twentieth century, based on Buddhist and Daoist teachings and practices.

human rights the basic rights and freedoms to which all humans are entitled, such as the right to food, shelter, education and protection by the law.

hydroelectric power electricity that is generated using the energy from running water.

import to bring in goods or materials from a foreign country for sale.

Islam a religion with belief in one god (Allah) and his last prophet, Muhammad.

martial arts the Asian arts of combat (fighting) or self-defence, such as karate, judo and aikido.

migrants people who move from one place to another to live or work.

organic made only from animal or vegetable materials, without any chemical substances.

raw materials unprocessed natural products, such as iron ore or coal.

resources things that are available to use, often to help develop a country's industry and economy. Resources could be minerals, workers (labour) or water.

textiles cloth or fabric, usually made from weaving.

Further information

Books

Changing World: China
by Jen Green
(Franklin Watts, 2008)

China (Country Insights)
by Julia Waterlow
(Wayland, 2006)

China (Eyewitness Guides)
by Hugh Sebag-Montefiore
(Dorling Kindersley, 2007)

China (World in Focus)
by Ali Brownlie Bojang
(Wayland, 2009)

Countries in the News: China
by Iris Teichmann
(Franklin Watts, 2009)

*Teens in China: Global
Connections*
by Karen Elizabeth Conyers
(Compass Point Books, 2007)

Websites

http://www.chinadaily.com.cn
China's English-language newspaper online.

http://china.org.cn
General information about China.

**http://www.cyberschoolbus.un.org/infonation/
index.asp**
United Nations website information about all
countries for children.

**http://news.bbc.co.uk/cbbcnews/hi/specials/
2005/china/default.stm**
Children's BBC Newsround China Special.

*Every effort has been made by the publisher to ensure
that these websites contain no inappropriate or offensive
material. However, because of the nature of the Internet,
it is impossible to guarantee that the contents of these sites
will not be altered. We strongly advise that Internet access
is supervised by a responsible adult.*

Index

Numbers in **bold** indicate pictures

A
Africa 15, **15**, 26, 27
astrology 19
Australia 14
B
banknotes 6
Beijing 7, 10, 14, 19, **27**
biofuels 15
Buddhism 16
C
Caribbean 15
Chinese communities overseas
   7, 13, 14, 15, 22
Christianity 16
cities 5, 8, 14, 15, 17, 19, 22, 28
Communism 24
companies 5, 15, 22, 23
Confucianism 16
Confucius 16, **16**
construction work **12**, **15**, 23
currency 7
D
Dalai Lama 25
Daoism 16
deserts 8, 10
Dongtan Eco-city 15, 28
E
earthquakes 10
economy 5, 20, 21, 22, 23, 28
education 13, 21
energy 11, 15, 26, 29
environment 8, 11, 28, 29
exports 5, 18, 20, 22
F
Falun Gong 16
farming 11, 15, 18, 21, 22, **22**, 24
flooding 10, **10**, 11
food 7, 13, 14, 15, 18, 23, 29

forests 11
France 5, 8
G
Germany 5, 28
government 13, 15, 16, 20, 24,
   25, 27
grandparents 13, **13**, 29
Great Wall of China 5, **23**
H
healthcare 12, 13, 21
Hu Jintao **26**
human rights 27
hydroelectric power 11
I
imports 6, 20, 22
India 12, 22
industry 6, 11, 21, 26
Islam 16
Italy 10
J
Japan 5, 28
L
labourers 15, **15**
Lhasa 8, **8**
M
Mao Zedong 24, **24**, 26
martial arts 19
media 27, **27**
medicine 17
Mongolia 10
mountains 8, 9
N
Nepal 9
O
Olympic Games 19, **19**
one-child policy 13, 29
P
Pakistan 9

pandas 11, **11**
paper 6, **6**
pasta 6, 18
population 4, 7, 12, 12, 13, 14,
   23, 28, 29
R
religion 16
resources 6, 26
rice 17, 18
rivers 8, 9, 11
S
services **20**, 21
Shanghai **4**, 9, 14, **21**
Sichuan province 10
size of China 4, 7, 8
sport 15, 19, **19**
T
Three Gorges Dam 11
Tibet 8, 25
Tibetan Plateau 8, **8**, 9
trade 9, 17, 20, 21, 26, 27
transport 9, 11, 15, 21, 22
U
UK 5, 12, 13, 14, 24
United Nations Security Council
   27
USA 5, 12, 13, 14, 21, 22, 24,
   26, 27, 28
W
work 13, 14, 15, 22
Y
Yangtze River (Chang Jiang) 9,
   10, 11, 15
Yangtze River dolphin 11
Yellow River (Huang He) 9, **9**, 10
Z
Zhangzhou **10**